Searchlight BOOKS™

How
Does Your
Body Work?

Your

Respiratory System

Judith Jango-Cohen

Lerner Publications Company
Minneapolis

▶ To Eliot, who still takes my breath away

Thanks to Sara Hoffmann, senior editor

Lerner Publications Company
A division of Lerner Publishing Group, Inc.
241 First Avenue North
Minneapolis, MN 55401 U.S.A.

Website address: www.lernerbooks.com

Library of Congress Cataloging-in-Publication Data

Jango-Cohen, Judith.
      Your respiratory system / by Judith Jango-Cohen.
          p.   cm. — (Searchlight books™—How does your body work?)
      Includes index.
      ISBN 978–0–7613–7451–0 (lib. bdg. : alk. paper)
       1. Respiratory organs—Juvenile literature. 2. Respiration—Juvenile literature.
   I. Title.
   QP121.J37 2013
   612.2—dc23   2011034278

Manufactured in the United States of America
1 – CG – 7/15/12

Contents

Chapter 1

THE NEED TO BREATHE

Imagine that you are sleeping.
Your chest floats up and down.
Quietly, your breath flows in and out.

You breathe slowly when you are asleep. How do you breathe when you run fast?

Next, imagine that you are running a race. Your mouth sucks in air. Your nostrils stretch wide. At the finish line, you drop onto the grass. As you gasp for breath, your chest pumps up and down.

You breathe faster when you run than when you rest.

Have you ever wondered why your breathing changes? When you are relaxed, you take slow, shallow breaths. When you are active, you gulp fast, deep breaths. The more energy you use, the more air you need. But what does breathing have to do with energy?

ENERGY COMES FROM FOOD. WHEN YOU EAT FOOD, YOU PUT ENERGY INTO YOUR BODY.

Energy and Breathing

Energy is locked up inside the food you eat. The air you breathe lets this energy out. Air is made of different gases. The gas that lets the energy out of food is called oxygen.

You always need to breathe because you are always using energy. Even when you are asleep, your heart is beating and your brain is working. How much oxygen you need depends upon how much energy you use.

You need energy to run. But you also need energy to think.

When you breathe in, oxygen enters your body. Food is in your body too. Oxygen combines with the food. Then energy is given off. A gas called carbon dioxide is also given off. Carbon dioxide is harmful. You must quickly get rid of it. The carbon dioxide goes into your lungs so you can breathe it out.

The more active you are, the faster you breathe. You take in more oxygen and give off more carbon dioxide.

After you run hard, you have to catch your breath. Your body needs more oxygen. It also has to get rid of lots of carbon dioxide.

The Respiratory System

Many parts of your body help you to breathe. These body parts are called the respiratory system. Most of the time, you are not thinking about breathing. But your respiratory system still works. You may be in school running a race. Or you may be in bed dreaming about winning one.

Your body has different systems to help you breathe, move, and digest your food. These systems all work together so you can do things like play basketball.

Chapter 2

NOSE AND THROAT

Your nose is like the door to your respiratory system. Most of the air that you breathe goes in through your nose.

But what happens when you have a cold and your nose gets clogged? Then you have to breathe through your mouth. Your mouth is like an emergency entrance. You use it when your nose is blocked or when you need extra air.

Usually you breathe through your nose. How do you breathe if your nose is clogged?

Your Nose: A Better Way to Breathe

Breathing through your nose is healthier than breathing through your mouth. Your nose cleans dust and germs out of the air you breathe. Hairs in your nose snag dust. Dust also gets stuck in mucus. Mucus is a slimy liquid that coats the inside of your nose. Germs are too small for the hairs to catch. But they stick to the mucus. Germs trapped in your nose do not enter your body to make you sick.

If you breathe in too much dust, you may have to sneeze! Sneezing blows dust out of your nose.

Mucus does more than trap dirt and germs. Mucus is wet. So mucus moistens the air you breathe. Air breathed in through your nose does not dry out your throat.

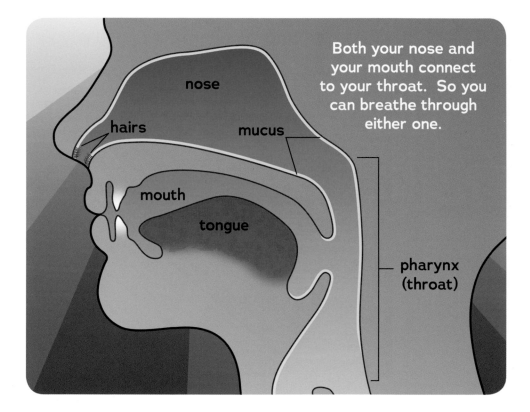

nose

hairs

mucus

Both your nose and your mouth connect to your throat. So you can breathe through either one.

mouth

tongue

pharynx (throat)

Besides cleaning and moistening the air, your nose also heats it. Your nose is warm. Air is heated as it flows through your nose. Even frosty air is warmed. This keeps the air from chilling your body.

When you play outside in the winter, your nose warms the air you breathe. This way, freezing air does not enter your throat and lungs.

The Pharynx and the Larynx

Cleaned, moistened, and warmed air goes from your nose into your throat. Another name for your throat is your pharynx. Air breathed in through your mouth enters the pharynx too. So do food and drink.

The lower part of the pharynx splits into two tubes. One tube connects to the stomach. This is where the food and liquids go. The other tube leads to the lungs. This is where the air goes. This tube for the air is called the larynx.

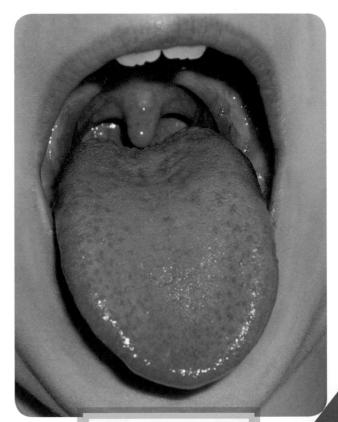

Your pharynx is behind your mouth.

Chapter 3

THE LARYNX

Both food and air travel down your pharynx. But then they go in different directions. Food moves down to your stomach. Air enters your larynx and heads for your lungs. Have you ever wondered how this happens without a mix-up?

Your pharynx carries both food and air into your body. But where do food and air go after they enter the pharynx?

Keep a Lid on It

Try to swallow and breathe at the same time. You cannot do it! When you swallow, a flap closes over your larynx. It fits like the lid on a box. The flap keeps you from breathing. Put your fingers on your neck while you swallow slowly. You can feel your larynx press up against your tongue while the flap closes.

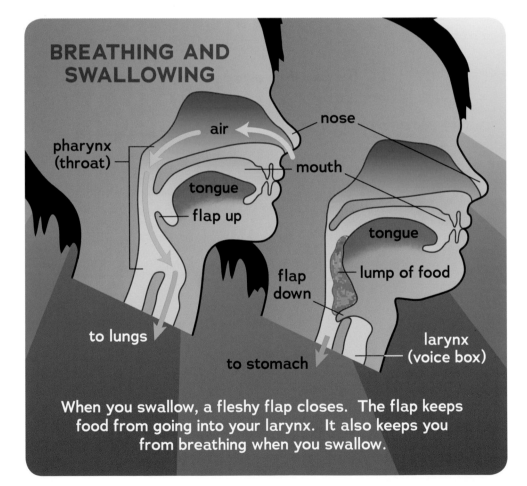

BREATHING AND SWALLOWING

nose

air

pharynx (throat)

mouth

tongue

flap up

tongue

lump of food

flap down

to lungs

to stomach

larynx (voice box)

When you swallow, a fleshy flap closes. The flap keeps food from going into your larynx. It also keeps you from breathing when you swallow.

Since your larynx is covered when you swallow, food cannot go into it. Food heads safely down the tube to your stomach.

But when you talk or laugh, your larynx is not covered. If you talk while eating, food may accidentally fall into your larynx. This blocks your larynx and makes you choke. Right away you start to cough. Coughing sends bursts of air upward through your larynx. The air knocks the food out. Once your larynx is unblocked, you can breathe again.

Talking with food in your mouth is dangerous. Food may go down the wrong way, causing you to choke.

Vocal Cords

Air flowing through your larynx passes between two stretchy bands called vocal cords. When you breathe, your vocal cords lie loosely against the sides of your larynx.

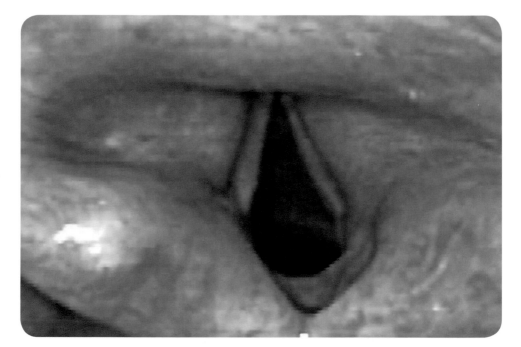

THIS PICTURE SHOWS A PERSON'S LARYNX AND VOCAL CORDS. THE SPACE BETWEEN YOUR VOCAL CORDS LETS AIR PASS THROUGH SO YOU CAN BREATHE.

When you speak, muscles pull your vocal cords together. This leaves only a small slit between them. Air moving through the slit makes the vocal cords vibrate, or shake. To feel your vocal cords vibrating, place your fingers on your neck. Then talk, hum, or sing.

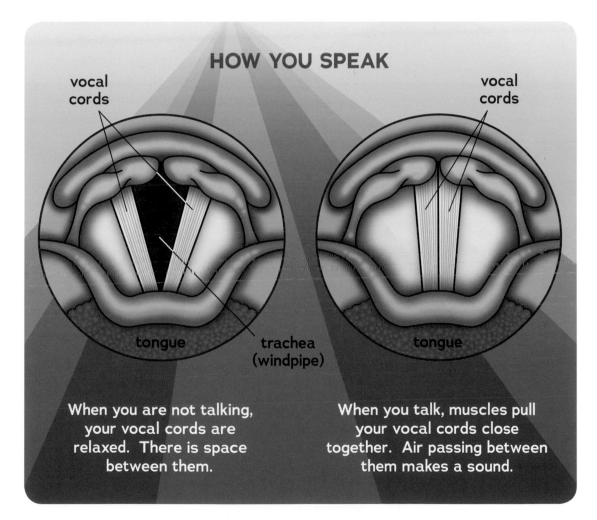

HOW YOU SPEAK

vocal cords

vocal cords

tongue

trachea (windpipe)

tongue

When you are not talking, your vocal cords are relaxed. There is space between them.

When you talk, muscles pull your vocal cords close together. Air passing between them makes a sound.

When your vocal cords vibrate, they make sounds. The tighter the vocal cords are stretched, the higher the sound is. You can see how this works. Pluck a rubber band as you stretch it tighter and tighter. Listen to how the sound changes.

A guitar's strings are attached to pegs. The pegs can be turned to make the strings tighter or looser. Then the sound the strings make becomes higher or lower. Vocal cords work in a similar way.

Small vocal cords make higher sounds than big vocal cords. Children have smaller vocal cords than adults have. So children have higher voices than adults. As you grow, your vocal cords get bigger. And your voice becomes lower.

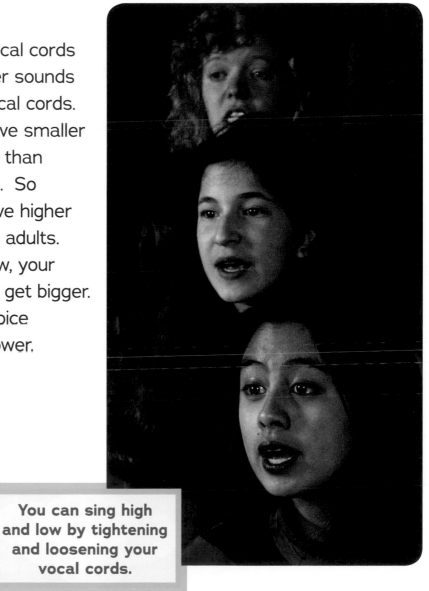

You can sing high and low by tightening and loosening your vocal cords.

Chapter 4

FROM LARYNX TO LUNGS

Your larynx is connected to a tube called the trachea. Muscles and stiff bands line the walls of the trachea. If food falls through your larynx and into your trachea, the muscles of the trachea tighten around it. This stops the food from going down into your lungs.

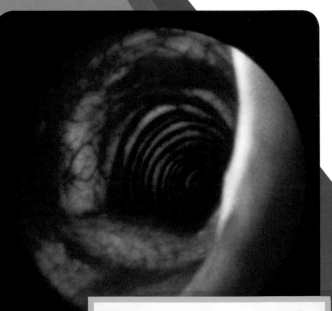

This picture shows the tube that is below the larynx. How do muscles in this tube protect your lungs?

Bronchi

The bottom part of your trachea divides into two branches. One branch goes to the right lung. The other branch goes to the left lung. These tubes that go to your lungs are called bronchi.

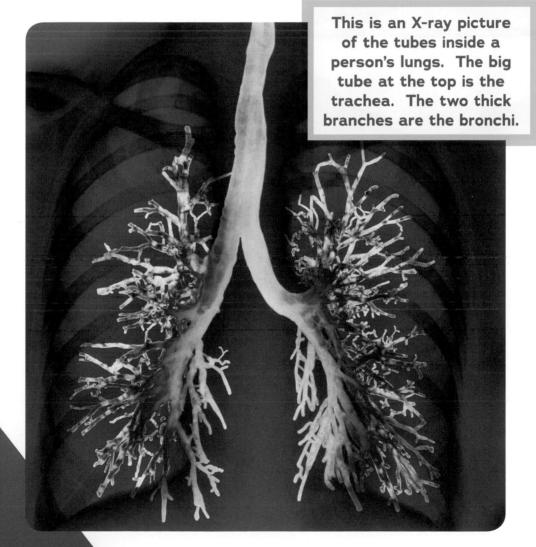

This is an X-ray picture of the tubes inside a person's lungs. The big tube at the top is the trachea. The two thick branches are the bronchi.

Your bronchi make mucus. The mucus traps dirt and germs that were not caught by the mucus in your nose. That way, they do not go into your lungs. But the bronchi must get rid of the dirty mucus. Otherwise, more and more mucus would build up. The bronchi would get clogged. You would not be able to breathe.

THE WALLS OF THE BRONCHI ARE
MADE OF DIFFERENT KINDS OF CELLS.
SOME OF THE CELLS MAKE MUCUS.

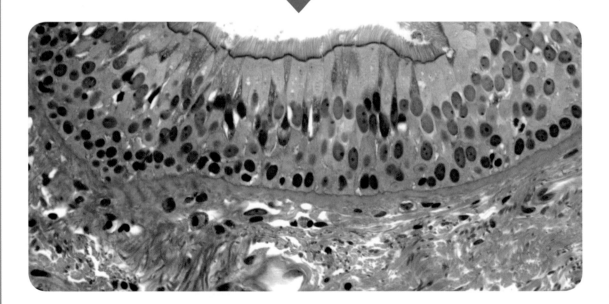

Tiny hairs in the bronchi get rid of the dirty mucus. The hairs are called cilia. The cilia wave back and forth like paddles. Cilia push the mucus up and away from your lungs. When the mucus reaches your pharynx, you can cough it out. You can also swallow it. Chemicals in your stomach destroy the germs trapped in the mucus.

Cilia look like tiny, waving hairs.

On to the Lungs!

Air has traveled from nose or mouth to pharynx, larynx, trachea, and bronchi. It has been cleaned, moistened, and warmed. It is ready to be delivered to your lungs.

Always try to cough into your elbow. This stops germs in the mucus from going into the air.

Chapter 5

THE LUNGS

Inside your lungs, the bronchi divide into smaller and smaller tubes. The tiniest of these tubes are called bronchioles. Bronchioles are a bit smaller across than the millimeter spaces on a ruler. Each bronchiole connects to a bundle of alveoli. Alveoli look like tiny balloons. Millions of bronchioles and alveoli are packed together in your lungs.

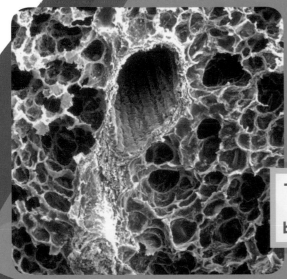

These are bronchioles. What does each bronchiole connect to?

Protective Bones

You cannot feel your lungs when you touch the center of your chest. Instead, you feel the flat bone that protects them. Connected to this bone are your ribs. Your ribs surround your lungs like a cage. Behind your lungs, your ribs connect to your backbone. Your backbone also helps protect your lungs.

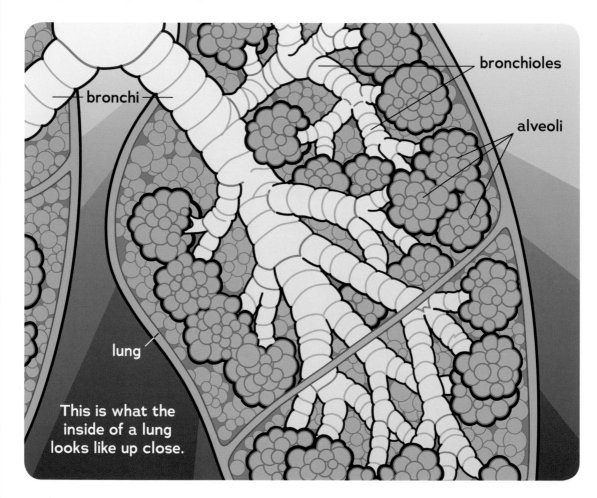

bronchi

bronchioles

alveoli

lung

This is what the inside of a lung looks like up close.

Diaphragm

Your chest also has many muscles. All these muscles move whenever you breathe. Below your lungs is a big, dome-shaped muscle called the diaphragm. The diaphragm separates your chest from your belly.

Your diaphragm helps you to take a big breath so you can blow out candles.

Take your deepest breath and hold it. Can you feel your diaphragm tighten? The diaphragm is pushing downward. This gives your lungs more room in your chest. Air rushes into this extra space when you breathe in.

Now let the air out slowly. When you breathe out, your diaphragm relaxes. When the diaphragm relaxes, it takes up more room. Your lungs are squeezed into a smaller space. The air is pushed out.

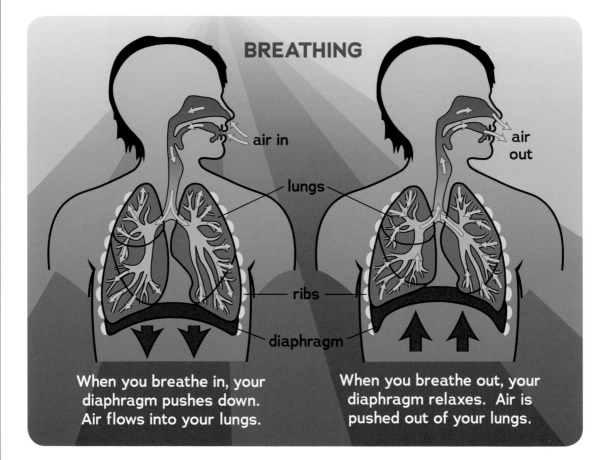

BREATHING

air in

air out

lungs

ribs

diaphragm

When you breathe in, your diaphragm pushes down. Air flows into your lungs.

When you breathe out, your diaphragm relaxes. Air is pushed out of your lungs.

> **When you take a deep breath, your ribs move up and out. This makes room for more air in your lungs.**

Other Muscles

Muscles between your ribs move along with your diaphragm. They lift your rib cage away from your lungs when you breathe in. This gives your lungs more room. Put your fingers on your ribs as you take a breath. Notice that your ribs move outward and up. When you breathe out, your ribs move down and in.

Your lungs are oxygen's last stop in your respiratory system. From your lungs, oxygen travels to every part of your body.

Chapter 6

AROUND THE BODY

Oxygen moves from your lungs to the rest of your body by entering your blood. Each of the alveoli in your lungs is surrounded by capillaries. Capillaries are tiny blood vessels. When oxygen leaves the alveoli, it passes into the blood in the capillaries. The blood carries the oxygen to your heart. Your heart pumps the oxygen-filled blood around your body.

The alveoli in the lungs look like tiny balloons. How does oxygen get from the alveoli to the rest of the body?

Oxygen, Energy, and Carbon Dioxide

Then the oxygen leaves the blood. It enters all the cells of your body. In the cells, oxygen combines with food to release energy. But carbon dioxide gas is also released. It passes out of the cells and into the capillaries. Flowing blood carries the carbon dioxide away.

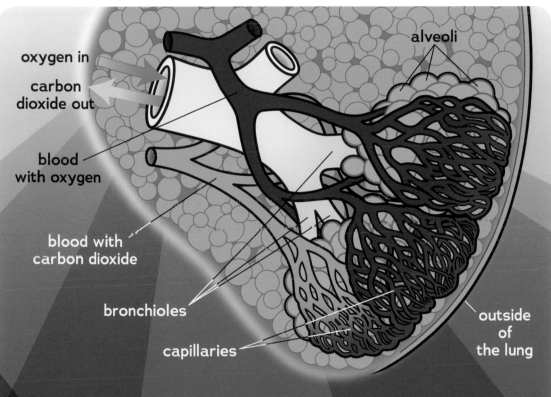

oxygen in

carbon dioxide out

blood with oxygen

blood with carbon dioxide

bronchioles

capillaries

alveoli

outside of the lung

Alveoli are surrounded by capillaries. Each time you breathe in, oxygen goes from the alveoli into the capillaries. Carbon dioxide from the capillaries goes into the alveoli. When you breathe out, you get rid of the carbon dioxide.

The blood and carbon dioxide soon reach your heart. The heart pumps them to the capillaries in your lungs. In your lungs, carbon dioxide passes out of the capillaries and into the alveoli. When you breathe out, carbon dioxide leaves the alveoli. It travels into the bronchioles, the bronchi, the trachea, the larynx, and the pharynx. Then it goes out through your nose or mouth.

When you breathe out, you get rid of carbon dioxide.

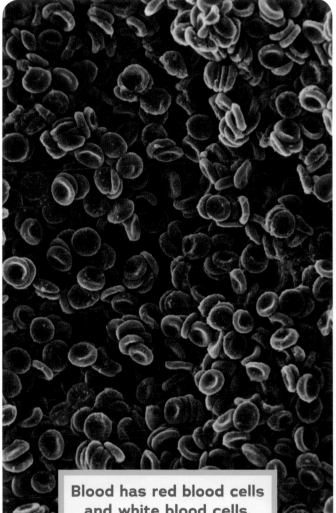

Blood has red blood cells and white blood cells. This picture shows red blood cells. Red blood cells carry oxygen through the body.

Working Together

Your respiratory system never stops working. It brings in oxygen and gets rid of carbon dioxide. But your respiratory system does not work alone. It needs the help of your heart and blood vessels. They move oxygen and carbon dioxide swiftly around your body.

Your Body: A Very Busy Place

A lot is happening inside you. Muscles in your chest are tightening and relaxing. Gases are moving through tubes and alveoli and into your blood. Your heart is pushing blood through your body. You are using energy.

Were you thinking about all this? You probably thought you were just relaxing and reading a book!

YOUR RESPIRATORY SYSTEM WORKS ON ITS OWN. IF IT DIDN'T, YOU WOULD ALWAYS HAVE TO THINK ABOUT BREATHING!

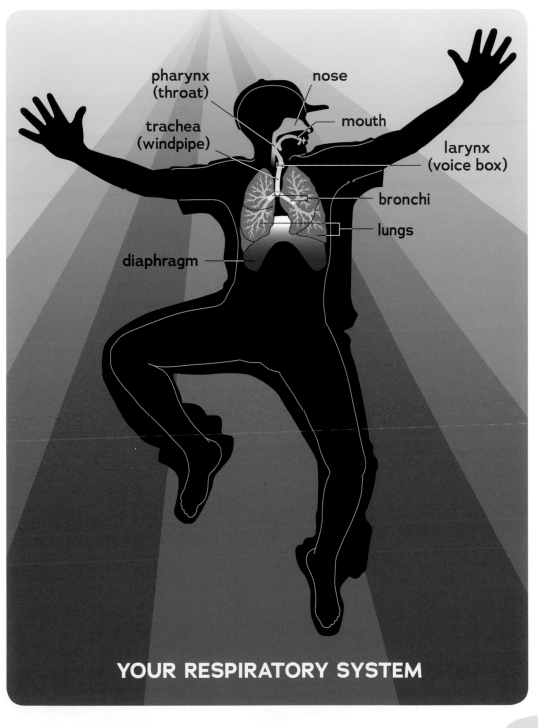

pharynx
(throat)

nose

mouth

trachea
(windpipe)

larynx
(voice box)

bronchi

lungs

diaphragm

YOUR RESPIRATORY SYSTEM

Glossary

alveoli: tiny, air-filled pouches in the lungs

bronchi: the two tubes that connect the windpipe to the lungs

bronchiole: a tiny tube inside the lungs

capillary: a tiny blood vessel. Capillaries surround each of the alveoli in the lungs.

carbon dioxide: the gas that is made when oxygen combines with food

cell: the building block of a living thing

cilia: tiny hairs in the air passages. Cilia wave back and forth like paddles to push mucus toward the throat.

diaphragm: the dome-shaped muscle below the lungs that is used in breathing

larynx: the voice box. A flap closes over the larynx when you swallow.

lungs: spongy sacks in the chest that put oxygen into the blood and take carbon dioxide out of it

mucus: a thick, sticky liquid that traps germs and dirt in the air passages

oxygen: the gas that combines with food to release energy

pharynx: the throat. Passages from the nose and mouth connect to the pharynx.

ribs: bones that surround the lungs like a cage

trachea: the windpipe. The trachea connects the larynx to the bronchi.

vocal cords: two stretchy bands inside the voice box that vibrate and make voice sounds

Learn More about the Respiratory System

Books

Gray, Susan H. *Living with Cystic Fibrosis*. Chanhassen, MN: Child's World, 2003. This informative book explains what it's like to live with cystic fibrosis, a disease that affects the respiratory system.

Larsen, C. S. *Crust & Spray: Gross Stuff in Your Eyes, Ears, Nose, and Throat*. Minneapolis: Millbrook Press, 2010. Would you like to learn about the gross and funny side of science? Then check out this entertaining look at mucus, phlegm, and other icky stuff related to your respiratory system.

Storad, Conrad J. *Your Circulatory System*. Minneapolis: Lerner Publications Company, 2013. Read about another important body system—the circulatory system—and find out how it works together with your respiratory system to keep your body working well.

Taylor-Butler, Christine. *The Respiratory System*. New York: Children's Press, 2008. Taylor-Butler discusses the respiratory system in this fun and educational book.

Websites

IMCPL Kids' Info Guide: Respiratory System
http://www.imcpl.org/kids/guides/health/respiratorysystem.html
This page from the Indianapolis Marion County Public Library has a list of resources you can use to learn more about the respiratory system.

Inside the Human Body: The Respiratory System
http://www.lung.ca/children/index_kids.html
This website has lots of information, plus activities and games.

KidsHealth: How the Body Works
http://kidshealth.org/kid/htbw/htbw_main_page.html
Click on the lungs to watch a movie, read articles, and try activities related to this important body part.

LERNER

Expand learning beyond the printed book. Download free, complementary educational resources for this book from our website, www.lerneresource.com.

SOURCE

Index

Photo Acknowledgments

The images in this book are used with the permission of: Image Source Royalty Free Images,
p. 4; © Monkey Business Images/Shutterstock.com, p. 5; © Royalty Free/CORBIS, pp. 6, 7, 8, 9,
21, 29; © Gleb Semenjuk/Shutterstock.com, p. 10; © Mandy Godbehear/Shutterstock.com, p. 11;
© Laura Westlund/Independent Picture Service, pp. 12, 16, 19, 28, 30, 33, 37; © Alaska Stock/
Alamy, p. 13; © Todd Strand/Independent Picture Service, pp. 14, 26; © Zurijeta/Shutterstock.
com, p. 15; © Echo/Cultura/Getty Images, p. 17; © Photo Researchers/Getty Images, p. 18;
© formiktopus/Shutterstock.com, p. 20; © CNRI/Photo Researchers, Inc., p. 22; © Innerspace
Imaging/Photo Researchers, Inc., p. 23; © Dr. Gladden Willis/Visuals Unlimited, Inc., p. 24; © SPL/
Photo Researchers, Inc., p. 25; © Biophoto Associates/Photo Researchers, Inc., p. 27; © Photodisc/
Getty Images, p. 31; © Lester V. Bergman/CORBIS, p. 32; © Meg Takamura/Getty Images, p. 34;
© Yorgos Nikas/Stone/Getty Images, p. 35; © iStockphoto.com/phi2, p. 36.

Front cover: © CLIPAREA/Custom Media/Shutterstock.com.

Main body text set in Adrianna Regular 14/20.
Typeface provided by Chank.